Tools in Nature

by Catherine Casey

illustrated by Tamara Anegon

Hi, I'm Cara and I'm a wildlife **photographer**. I take photos of animals in the wild. I use tools to help me do my job.

Binoculars help me to see animals far away.
Then I take photographs using my camera.
The tripod helps to hold my camera still.

Tools for Food

People used to think only humans used tools. However, animals use tools, too! Chimpanzees use sticks to find food.

This smart chimp uses a stick to collect termites.

They poke sticks into **termite** mounds. Termites bite the stick. Then the crafty chimps gobble them up.

Crows use sticks to fish for insects. Crows hold the stick in their beak. Then they poke insects hiding in tree bark.

The insects bite the stick. The crow pulls the stick out. It gets an insect treat.

Another animal that uses tools is the sea otter. It needs to get to hidden food.

Sea otters eat **clams** and other shellfish. They use rocks to break open shells. Otters pound the shell against the rock until it breaks open.

Hold your noses – this one's a bit smelly! Burrowing owls that nest underground eat beetles. They use an odd tool to help catch the beetles.

Owls use animal dung as a tool. The owl puts the dung by their nest. It waits for the beetles to come out and sniff the dung. Then it dives.

Tools to Stay Safe

Some animals need to protect themselves from harm. They use tools to avoid threats.

Gorillas can use big rocks to appear **threatening**.

Researchers watched a gorilla wading into deep water. It used a stick to calculate the water's **depth**. Using the stick in this way kept the gorilla safe.

Orangutans also use tools to help them stay safe. Orangutans make an alarm call when they see predators.

Snakes stay away from the orangutan's threatening call.

Some clever orangutans hold a leaf in front of their mouth. This makes them sound deeper. They then seem bigger than they are to predators.

Some animals use things from their **surroundings** to protect themselves. Clever dolphins can do this.

Dolphins look for food in the sand. They use a soft sea animal to protect their beaks.

Octopuses perform a clever trick with coconut shells. They find shells that have been dropped in the sea.

The octopus blows the shell to clean out any mud. Then it uses the shell for shelter. It can also hide from bigger animals.

Tools for Comfort

Some animals use tools to keep dry and comfortable.

These bats make a leaf tent. The leaf protects them from the rain.

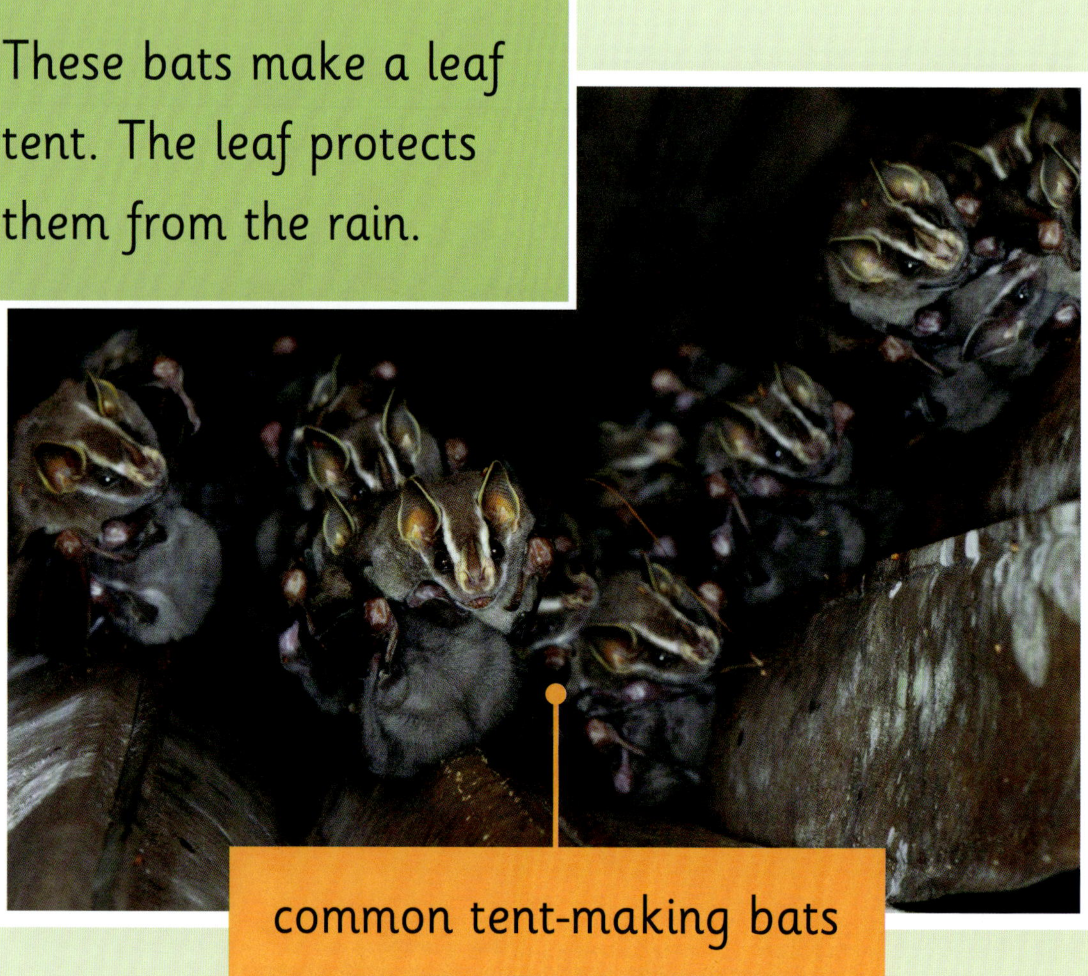

common tent-making bats

Elephants can even make their own tools! They pull off sticks and branches. They use them to **swat** away annoying insects.

This mother shows her baby how to scratch an itch.

Orangutans use leaves to keep themselves dry in the rain.

The tailorbird gets its name as it can stitch. It can make a pouch for its nest. It uses leaves and spider silk, or plant threads.

Glossary

clams: sea organisms that live in shells
depth: how deep something is
photographer: a person that takes photos with a camera
surroundings: the place around something
swat: to hit away
termites: insects that feed on wood or dead plants
threatening: something that is seen as frightening

Index